MW01181103

Contents

Introduction

Books about dating all face one of two problems: either the author is married, or the author is single. In the first case, it's too easy to think *'Well sure, that approach worked for you, but that's just one story.'* What if the married author has fallen out of touch, and he or she doesn't understand how things are these days? In the case of a single author, even more doubts arise: *How can I be sure whether any of this works, if it hasn't worked out for you?*

That kind of thinking assumes that the goal of dating is finding a spouse, which is true. However, even though the ultimate indicator of success in dating is marriage, there are plenty of ways to be successful without yet having found a spouse. This book will detail some of those ways [See "Why We Date"].

This very small book is meant as a practical guide to the early stages of dating. To maintain its usefulness, I will try to keep explanations brief and advice blunt. You don't have to read the book in order. If you think "Asking for a Date" will be the most useful section, jump straight there! For explanations that are discussed in other chapters, I will put "links" in brackets, just like in the last sentence of the paragraph above.

I write from my own experience and perspective—that of a young, single, Christian male—so this book is written primarily to young, Christian men. (That said, I feel non-Christians and females may still benefit from reading sections of this book.) I write as one who is still trying. Nobody wants to be good at first dates, because that means the dates aren't working! It's much better to get in the game, find who you're looking for, and get out, without having a lot of practice. But in terms of exploring compatibility with a number of women for whom I have much admiration and respect, I'd say I'm doing okay. I rarely avoid anyone out of embarrassment, and I have gained friendship with several awesome ladies. I can be honest, though, in saying I'd still prefer a wife over a number of new friends.

With this being a book of mostly practical advice (with some theology thrown in to back it all up), I think of it as an "80%" book: it will work for about 80% of the intended audience about 80% of the time. *But, you say, I don't want an "80%" relationship! I want something special!* My expectation is that what makes a relationship special is how it sneaks up and surprises you, and how it changes what makes sense to you and what doesn't. Even walking intentionally toward a dating relationship, I fully expect to be surprised by love. This book will attempt to cover part of the walking.

0.8 × 0.8 = 0.64 = 64%

There can be no pride in writing from a place where I'm still walking. I'm merely trying to make more peace for people like me. I see a lot of trouble and conflict in my generation from avoidable mistakes in dating. I see just as much trouble and conflict, if not more, from a fear of dating, especially among young people in the Church. I have hope that sharing my little experience may add to someone's peace and make life simpler for my young friends and for me.

In truth, you have probably already heard much of the wisdom contained in this book. It's a lot of common sense. The advice contained in this book is mostly simple, but I'm not foolish enough to call it easily-executed. Dating is hard! It takes guts, and work, and planning. It takes vulnerability and effort, and even effort to be vulnerable. But we don't want dating to be easy, we want dating to be *worth it.* I see the difficulty in dating firsthand on a somewhat regular basis, and for now, I see that difficulty as a very good thing. I hope that in addition to a book of advice, this would be an encouragement to my friends to face the difficulty of dating, to date boldly and to date well.

1. Why We Date

This section outlines a small portion of the theological basis for dating in general. It does not contain very much practical advice, but it will be referenced throughout the book. Feel free to skip this section, but be sure to come back if you ever find use of the last chapter, "Over It."

A man who finds a wife...

There are many scriptures that identify critical aspects of romantic relationships, but two stand out to me as fundamental truths for dating. The first comes from the book of Proverbs, which is a collection of practical wisdom from King Solomon and other authors for living life in a God-pleasing way. Some people consider Proverbs to be an "80%-style" book. Whereas the Apostle Paul writes in 1 Corinthians that it is good for some to stay single, the book of Proverbs offers Godly wisdom for most people, most days. In Proverbs, Solomon says:

> "A man who finds a wife finds a good thing
> and obtains favor from the Lord."
> Proverbs 18:22 HCSB

This verse almost makes me laugh for its clarity and simplicity. I love that there is nothing fancy or overly specific here. Should I look for a wife? Yes. The Bible says if I find a wife, I find a good thing! More than that, the Bible clarifies that a wife is a courier of "favor from the

Lord." By finding a wife, I meet a person who carries the goodness of God and shares that goodness with me directly.

I know almost nothing of the complexities and difficulties of married life. Based on my belief in God, I know that I want His favor, and I know that what He calls "a good thing" is indeed good. So I see that seeking out a wife is a worthwhile pursuit, even if it takes effort and heartache. Why do I date? That's how people find spouses in our culture, and finding a wife is finding a good thing.

Right now, I'm looking for my first real job. I believe what my parents and friends have told me—that having a job is a good thing. I have experienced the joy of hard work, and a job will offer me the opportunity to do good work as a part of everyday life. So I take part in the cultural structure that helps people like me find jobs. I go to job fairs and meet employers. I follow leads that friends and family give me when they see my skills might be compatible with a business they know. I proactively contact companies in a clear, professional way.

The same applies for dating! If you want a good thing—a wife—you participate in actively seeking one out through dating. Some people find great job opportunities in very non-traditional ways, and their friends rightly rejoice when it happens. But only a fool sits around waiting for a company to call him with a job offer.

I'll be honest: looking for a job stinks sometimes. It can be tiring and confusing. It's hard not to be down when companies don't respond how you think they should. But two things make dating *way* better than looking for a job. The first is that you never date alone; the second is that you only have to date once.

You have a team

Dating is the process of finding someone with whom you are compatible for marriage. The good news is that in every dating relationship, there are two people searching for spouses—the man and the woman. That means you and whomever you date are on a team! You get to help one another find spouses, primarily by evaluating whether you're right for each other. So you know that at minimum, one other person—the woman you're dating—is on your side in your search for a wife.

Thankfully, most people also have friends and relatives cheering them on in the pursuit of a marriage relationship. The more open and vulnerable I am in my pursuit of a wife, I've found, the more people want to help me find one.

I spent some time building a skin-on-frame canoe (picture a skeleton of a boat covered in water-proof fabric) over a break from school, and when I came back I had not finished it. The busyness of life got in the way of me making progress on it, until I found a great reason to work harder. There was a woman I really wanted to take on a date, and I thought paddling a canoe would make for a fun time. When my friends in the dorm noticed I had resumed building the canoe and asked why, I told them! Soon I had plenty of friends cheering me on to finish the canoe quickly (especially after we had chosen the day for the date!). A girl friend helped me cut the fabric skin for the canoe and start to attach it. A couple of guys stayed up late to help me stitch the ends. A few others risked sitting in the canoe with me to check if my craft was water-tight. It wasn't. My roommate made late-night trips to buy waterproofing spray, and got sticky attempting to apply it in high winds.

By the day of the date, a whole group of people had invested themselves in my life and in my pursuit of a good thing. Their care gave me confidence, and it made me feel loved and supported. Sure, there was a risk of them knowing if the relationship didn't work out, but the same people who supported me in my openness would not mock me in broken heartedness. They understood my goal, and they cheered me on.

Most people delight in joining your team, I've found, if you are open and sincere about your desire, and if you desire a good thing. At the very least, the woman that you have become vulnerable to in expressing your desire for marriage through dating is on your team, and she needs you on hers.

even if that means leaving that if it's not you

You only date once

The following saying has sustained me through some tough times and lifted the spirits of many of my friends:

"You only need enough game for one girl."

What a relief! That truth echoes in my head sometimes, gently humbling me. Looking at the entire "dating scene" overwhelms my senses; it's too much for me to handle. The fact above reminds me that I don't need to become a master of social interaction nor an expert in dating to be successful. In fact, as I discussed in the intro, I feel that if I became too much a seasoned veteran at first dates, I would necessarily be *un*successful.

More than that, the saying is a comforting thought for when a dating relationship does not end in marriage. *It didn't work out this time, but that's okay; it only has to work out one time.* I've said it as many times as I've heard it as an encouraging word from good friends. I'll talk about this more later [See "Over It"].

Ultimately, all that is required to be successful in dating is to know and to be known by one woman. If she's the one you want to commit to (and vice versa), then you're on to the next stage. Avoid being overwhelmed at the prospect of dating by remembering your mission: to find a good thing—a wife.

SMH

Before I discuss the second scripture that I find fundamental for dating, I will take a moment to discuss *bad* reasons to date. The two poor motivations for dating I hear most often basically boil down to 1) sexual contact and 2) fun.

Sex is a good thing. When I say sex, I mean sex and everything like it—physical expressions of mutual romantic affection. God created sex, and He called creation good, so *Nice syllogism* sex must be good! I believe that sex is designed to tie people together. (Apparently a bunch of scientists think so, too. Google "Oxytocin.") It's also for making babies.

I'm not an expert on sexual contact. I'd go so far as to say I'm the opposite. But this metaphor explains my understanding so far: dating for sex is like tying your shoelaces in tight, difficult knots every morning and then cutting them with scissors every evening. The shoelaces are your heart, and every occasion of sexual contact is another knot that can't be untied, but must be cut. After a series of ended relationships, you have damaged laces that you can't use quite as well. (Remember that your heart being tied to your wife's heart with sex is a good thing.)

You rarely want the hassle of cutting the knots, so you end up leaving your shoes on, even in stupid situations like taking a shower after you mow the yard. Look, it's not a perfect metaphor. All I'm saying is that sex and anything like it will tie your heart to another person, even if it's not a

9

person you think you *want* to be tied to. It will make you prolong relationships that aren't going anywhere, and convince you of things you know aren't true.

It's pretty clear, at least, that sex really complicates dating. It muddles your evaluation of a potential spouse with all kinds of emotions that are great within a marriage context and really inconvenient outside of one. Avoiding sexual contact makes breaking off a relationship much simpler, and it makes later encounters with a dating partner pleasant rather than awkward. I never have to run into someone I took on a date and think *Oh hey, I touched that person's mouth with my mouth.* The desire to avoid that thought follows from my desire to not be attached to a woman whom I don't want to date or marry. I want to prolong the time where I can think of who a woman is and how to continue getting to know her without the complication of a physical aspect of our relationship. C.S. Lewis says, "The truth is that wherever a man lies with a woman, there, whether they like it or not, a transcendental relation is set up between them which must be eternally *enjoyed* or *eternally endured*" (*The Screwtape Letters, Letter XVIII).* Anyone who denies the attachment brought about by sexual contact is lying (either to you, or to himself). If he is telling the truth about his own experience, he should mourn the loss of a good way to be attached to his future wife.

God has a way of making all things new though. God has abundant grace for everyone who asks Him for it. The same grace that frees us and makes us new also calls us to walk in freedom—freedom from all kinds of sin, including sexual sin. Make no mistake: when God commands people to enjoy sex how He designed it and to avoid every other use (1 Thes. 4:3), it's not just good advice. It's a requirement. But He wants to help us enjoy

[handwritten margin note: Little bit abrupt jump from sex to kissing]

10

sex and all its benefits in terms of relationships when we do it His way. Walk in wisdom, and err on the side of moving "too slow."

As a rule of thumb, I think physical expression of affection is allowable in the early stages of dating as long as it's in one direction (from you to her, and nothing in return). If you honestly say that you're kissing her so *she* feels affection and not so you feel affection (or something else), I will still ask you to double- and triple- and quadruple-check before giving it a thumbs up. About 99.9% of the time you're lying to yourself. If your body is preparing for sex, you can be sure you're lying to yourself. The extreme difficulty here arises first because most physical expressions of affection are two-directional, and second because you crave this type of contact in the most vulnerable parts of your humanness. There's a time for that two-way giving of love, but it's not now. The ability to give without wanting to receive can only be had by drilling down *deep* into your identity as one already loved, who doesn't need any more. But physical expression of affection is not an area to mess around in; it's deadly serious. Don't find out how far is too far by passing the edge of the slope and tumbling down. At most, stick to simple things: a quick kiss on the cheek, an embrace, an arm around the shoulders. At any rate, this book is for the early stages of dating, so you shouldn't be too worried about this anyway!

The second bad reason for dating that I hear most, even in my own family, is dating for "fun" or for "experience." It's difficult for me to express in writing how utterly stupid I find dating just "for fun" to be. When I hear this, I cringe so hard it hurts. First of all, most of the time when someone says they date for fun, they really mean they date for the reason I discussed above. But even if not, dating for fun is simply dumb. Make no mistake: dating *is* fun, and it's supposed to be. But to date only for fun and not to find a spouse—besides being a massive waste of time and emotional energy for both parties—only leads to unnecessary heartbreak.

It also doesn't help to date "for experience." If dating experience were necessary to find a spouse, we wouldn't hear stories of high school sweethearts who made it work and are still in love, or when we did hear those stories we would feel robbed rather than inspired.

You only need enough game for one woman, and you shouldn't be able to trick her into liking you with your impressive dating skills that you've gathered from all your "experience." When you find the woman you want to commit to, and when you find she wants to commit back, you'll know you've reached the right experience level. If you're reading this book to get tips on dating for fun, do me a favor and put it back on the shelf until you're ready to date "for real."

I will make one note to soften that last point: I think a lot of people say they're dating for fun because it's easier than saying "I'm dating to find a spouse." Think of how strange it would be to ask someone out not with a "I'd like to get to know you better," but with a "I'd like to check our compatibility for marriage." One of the wild things about dating is that it's a paradox: the purpose of dating is to find a spouse, but if I think of asking someone out on a date as a marriage proposal, I'll choke. So the easy way out is to tell everyone (including myself) that I'm dating just for fun, and in the back of my mind hope it works out with someone. I'll also say that fun is a pretty good indicator of compatibility early on; if I don't enjoy spending time with a woman, why would I keep asking her out? Even still, being vulnerable and honest with myself and with those around me, I believe, is the way to go.

Theology of dating

If I read this book six months ago, I would have been frustrated by the amount the author has mentioned vulnerability. The truth found in Genesis 1:26-27 and all of its implications have been unfolding in my life recently, and it has drastically shaped the way I view dating.

> 26 Then God said, "Let Us make man in Our image, according to Our likeness. They will rule the fish of the sea, the birds of the sky, the livestock, all the earth, and the creatures that crawl on the earth."

> 27 So God created man in His own image;
> He created him in the image of God;
> He created them male and female.

This text was written to the ancient Israelites to remind them of the deepest truths of God's character and of who He created humans to be.

Verse 26 says "'Let Us make man in Our image...'" To whom is God speaking that He would say "Us" and "Our"? God was not alone, and God was speaking to other Persons that had the right and the ability to "make." Certainly, God existed in relationship even before He made humans. This is critical, because the Bible says explicitly in 1 John what it shows throughout all of scripture: God is love. But love is always acted out in the context of a relationship; love is never a point, always a line. The fact that God existed eternally in powerful loving relationship reveals an aspect of His divine character: God delights in participating in loving relationship.

13

"So God created man in His own image." When Israelites heard the word "image," they would think of what you and I might call idols. Carved stone and wood idols in ancient Near Eastern religions represented the presence of pagan gods. God essentially sets up the impressively intricate human images He made to "rule... all the earth" next to these motionless stone idols and says, "Those dead, mute, powerless carved images represent dead, mute, powerless gods. You living, loving, powerful humans represent Me, the living, loving, powerful God." Humans are made in God's image, representing to one another and to all creatures God's divine character.

We distort God's image in us any time we act in way that is not aligned with God's nature. Since God is love, any distortion of His image in us is a rejection of love; as distorted images we can't love God as we were made to, and we can't love each other as we were made to.

God let His desire for relationship *affect* Him so much that He acted. God so desired loving relationship with humans that He sent His Son Jesus, who is "the image of the invisible God" (Col. 1:15). Jesus perfectly bears the resemblance of God. This historical person named Jesus of Nazareth, who is fully God, let Himself be affected by all the distorted humans around Him, compassionately healing them and teaching them. But we humans hated God so much that we sought to destroy His image, His Son. Jesus let Himself be affected by His love for humans, even to the point that He let us kill Him.

Little did we know, however, that God would use our hatred to draw us back into loving relationship with Him. See, when an image gets distorted so much that it doesn't look anything like the subject it supposedly resembles, there's nothing to be done. It can't just be polished and sanded. The image has to be destroyed and remade. Jesus, as the perfect image of God, came to restore all the images of God in the world. He came to show us how to bear God's image again, to love rightly. Even though He was the totally undistorted Image of God, He showed us how to be destroyed by dying on a cross, and how to be remade by getting back up out of the grave on the third day after His burial. This resurrection could only be accomplished by God's power, and Jesus invites us to be destroyed and remade by believing in Him and trusting Him with our whole lives.

Be Affected

So we see in God's character such a profound desire to be in loving relationship that He would let Himself be affected by His love for us. God was willingly affected, even to the point of stepping down among creatures who hated Him, even to the point of death. His affectedness was the very means by which our loving relationship with God was restored! As bearers of God's image, we too ought to be affected by our desire for relationship. Humans should let themselves be so affected by desire for all kinds of loving relationship that it demands action. I think God gave us a hint in Genesis 1:27 to specifically desire relationship between male and female as a way of bearing His image.

I believe that at the deepest level, this is why we date. God handcrafted us to desire loving relationship, including a special relationship between male and female, and to be so affected by that desire that we would act on it in amazing ways. By moving toward love, we participate in our purpose as images of God, which is the very best thing we can do in life.

15

Breathe

That was kind of a lot, I know. But I think it tracks with our existing understanding of love. Think about how we got the word "affection"; it must have come from someone recognizing how "affected" they were by their desire for another person. When I show affection for loved ones, I'm showing them how much I let them affect me. Dating is being affected by and acting on my deep desire for a marriage relationship with a woman.

The theology and logic of why we date is mostly out of the way; let's get to the practical advice. Tip number one: dating well is all about confidence. Who hasn't heard that before? Be careful! Our society thinks confidence comes from puffing your chest and jutting your chin even when you feel nervous; that is not so. Confidence in dating (as in life) comes from knowing the truth and resting in it. You just read biblical truth about why dating is a good thing to do. If you believe that truth, take a deep breath, and let's get walking.

2. Asking for a Date: Clarity is Key

As the title of this section may suggest, clarity is the key to doing well in asking a woman on a date. So you found someone on your radar that's just too interesting to leave un-asked. Here's how to ask her out clearly (and why it's important):

Use your voice

I'll say it clearly here so you don't hear it unclearly anywhere else: asking a woman on a first date by text is simply unacceptable. The tone of a conversation matters. With acquaintances, text is acceptable for conveying factual information. "When/where is the meeting?" "Is class cancelled?" These are great questions to be handled over text. But the lack of tone conveyed in a text is seriously problematic, especially when communicating with someone who doesn't know you well enough to read your intended tone into every message. Texting is the number one sponsor of good dating's biggest enemy: ambiguity.

Ambiguity is not to be confused with mystery! With any initial interest, there should be a healthy amount of curiosity. Curiosity requires some level of mystery; if I think I know everything about a woman, then there's nothing left for me to be curious about. Curiosity is made out of 1) a lack of knowledge, and 2) a desire to know. As humans are extremely complex and constantly changing beings, there will always be more for me to find out about

17

my love interest. I never have to worry about mystery as long as my desire to know remains.

Problems start when people try to generate fake mystery through ambiguity, in an effort to cause curiosity. I just explained how the first ingredient of curiosity will never run out on its own; there's no use trying to stir up curiosity by faking the first ingredient, when you're really just scared that the second ingredient, the desire to know, is missing. Middle school boys have been using text to cause ambiguity with girls at least since I was in seventh grade. Some boys never grew out of it.

Be bold. Use your voice to ask her out. That means text messaging is unacceptable. A phone call is allowable. The less-bold side of me likes to call when it comes to dating, because I get to use my voice, but there's a decent chance I don't have to speak with the woman directly. Who answers the phone these days? I just leave a voicemail. Phone calls are also very useful when I'm interested in a woman whom I rarely see in passing.

Even better than text (which is unacceptable) and phone call is asking in-person. Yes. In the same way that tone adds an essential element to written communication, body language adds an important element to verbal communication. This takes some serious guts, but a woman you want to date will appreciate it.

Say the word "date"

No woman who likes you will say no to a date because you were too clear in asking her out. However, a woman who is unsure whether she likes you may be flattered enough by your openness and clarity to give it a shot. Ultimately, you ask a woman out to check whether you get along well and like spending time together, so it's better to find out than to leave things ambiguous.

Here's a tough truth: a woman who does not have any romantic interest in you simply *doesn't*. You will not be able to trick someone into having romantic interest in you in the long term, and you don't want to. For her sake and yours, it's better to be clear and vulnerable with your intentions and to date with the confidence which that requires.

If you ask <u>with ambiguity</u>, the conversation between her and her friends goes one of two ways:

1) *She likes you/ would be open to going on a date*
   Crush: (apprehensive) I think [insert your name here] might be asking me out!
   Friend: Well how do you know?! What did he say?
   Crush: He asked what I was doing this weekend then asked if I wanted to "hang out."
   Friend: Is it a date? Do you want it to be?
   Crush: I don't really know... Maybe! I guess I'll just go and see what it's like!
   [Note: Based on instances between my sister and my mother, this conversation loops for no less than half an hour. Sentences are remembered and analyzed and re-remembered and re-analyzed. It's a whole thing.]

2) *She's not that into you and she knows it*
   Crush: (apprehensive) I think [insert your name here] might be asking me out...
   Friend: Well how do you know?! What did he say?
   Crush: He asked what I was doing this weekend then asked if I wanted to "hang out."
   Friend: Is it a date? Do you want it to be?

Crush: I don't really know… I hope not! Ugh, I don't want to be mean, I just don't like him. I hope he gets a hint; I'll just say I'm busy again.

Asking with clarity, you basically have nothing to lose and everything to gain. It may be that you want to avoid the embarrassment of rejection, and you think you can only be rejected if you actually ask. Here are two reasons why that doesn't make sense. First, you have confidence, not from pride, but from knowing that asking a woman on a date is a good thing [See "Why We Date"]; letting your embarrassment overrule your confidence can only cause loss and not gain. If you let fear of embarrassment keep you from asking, you definitely will not get a date. If you walk in humble confidence and push through the fear of embarrassment, you might get a date with a great woman. In the words of Michael Scott, in the words of Wayne Gretzky, "You miss 100% of the shots you don't take." Setting down your pride—and the fear of embarrassment that pride causes—definitely falls into the category of "simple, but not easy."

The second reason that attempting to avoid the embarrassment of rejection through ambiguity does not make sense is that it simply doesn't work. Look back to the second conversation above. It stinks finding out your crush doesn't like you back, but it is much worse to have someone you admire dread hearing from you because of the anxiety caused by ambiguity. You will not earn her affection this way. Contrary to popular belief and "popular" culture, persistence is usually viewed as creepy rather than endearing. You don't want to be the creepy guy who doesn't take a hint. I've been the creepy guy who doesn't take a hint; it only leads to much deeper embarrassment than could ever come from getting rejected in asking for a date. It leads to excessive reading into every communication and interaction. It's unhealthy. The problem here incubates in denial—if I can convince myself there might be chance, then I'll try to prolong the interactions and hope she'll come around. Be honest with yourself. If you keep attempting to hang out, that means you have romantic interest. If she is always busy and makes no proactive attempts to reschedule, she doesn't like you. I repeat: you don't want to be the creepy guy who can't take a hint [More on this in "Over It"].

How do we break out? How do we fight denial? Ask the woman on a date with clarity. I feel my shoulders relaxing as I transition from the above to what's next. I'm going to repeat the conversations from above, except in the aftermath of a man asking a woman on a date with clarity.

3) *She likes you/ would be open to going on a date*
Crush: [Insert your name here] just asked me out!
Friend: Wait, what?! How do you know?! What did he say?
Crush: He said "I'd like to take you on date this weekend!" I'm freaking out! I said yes! We're doing coffee!
Friend: Woah! I didn't even know he liked you! This is exciting! What are you going to wear?!

4) *She's not that into you and she knows it*
Crush: Aww, [Insert your name here] just asked me out.
Friend: Wait, what?! How do you know?! What did he say?
Crush: He said "I'd like to take you on date this weekend."

Friend: Are you going?!
Crush: I don't think so; I respect him a lot, but I only like him as a friend. I told him no.
Friend: Ah okay. But dang! Respect for him just asking you out like that!
Crush: I know! I'm flattered. — Is this fair?

Now that's better. If you got the first of those two results, fantastic! If you got the second, it stinks, but it's still good. The bottom line is a woman who likes you will say yes if you ask with clarity; a woman who does not like you will not start liking you if you go with ambiguity. It is better by far to know where you stand and to keep moving than it is to agonize over every detail.

Best of all, a woman who is unsure of her feelings toward you may agree to a date simply because she feels honored to be asked. I guarantee you that I've had the chance to go on dates with women who are *way* out of my league because I was direct in asking. I wasn't even smooth! One time, after meeting a woman at a banquet and running into her a couple of times through church and friends, I decided to ask her out. As we were parting ways in the parking lot of In-N-Out Burger, standing about 12 feet apart (take a second to think about how awkward that distance is), I said a little too loudly "Can we go on a date?" Yikes. She turned and smiled, and walked a few steps closer, and agreed to go. Now if directness makes up for awkwardness, I'm all in, because I need all the help I can get.

Clarity in asking people out on dates is lacking in our culture, and the easiest way to be clear is to use the word "date." There will be no doubts about your intentions, and she'll feel no uneasiness in wondering about them. She'll feel honored to be asked. She may say no, and that's alright. It's better to know than to not know. She may say yes, and that's when you celebrate with your boys and skip to chapter 3 [See "Planning a Date"]. Alternate phrases that are not quite as good as using the word "date" include:

- "I'd like to buy you (dinner, coffee, etc.)."
- "Can I take/treat you to (event, meal, etc.)?"
- "I'd like to get to know you better. Would you be up for (propose date idea)?"

If you know you like her, or even if you *think* you like her, calling something that you treat as a date a "hangout" is unacceptable. How hurt would you be if you asked a girl on a date with clarity and she agreed, and then on your way to pick her up she texted you "Hey can I bring a friend to our hangout today?" It would be totally unfair! The opposite is also true. Asking someone to "hang out" when you know you wish it were a date is disrespectful. It's also a waste of time and emotional energy. Be fair, be bold, be clear.

My personal favorite way of asking remains the rough-cut and un-sanded: "Can I take you on a date?" This brand of counter-cultural clarity conveys confidence— confidence that you're sure you want to know her better, and that you're sure dating is a good thing. I personally believe that clarity in asking women out will lead to more peace in our generation, especially in the Church.

Ask her soon

Here's a problematic scenario that may be familiar to you (especially if you are involved in college ministry): A man meets a woman and she's *perfect*. He wants to ask her on a date but he takes a while to build up the courage. For weeks and months, he thinks of how great it will be when everything works out. Eventually, some occasion is poetic enough for him to act. He says to her "I think we need to talk…" (*never* use an ellipse like that). He confesses his grand feelings for her, and she's totally blindsided, as this is the first time she's hearing about it. Of course, she's not ready for the emotional involvement he just described. He leaves heartbroken, and she leaves upset for apparently breaking the heart of a friend.

Now, many of us have heard of conversations like this going well; remember that this is an 80% book, for practical wisdom and peace in dating. The strategy of the man I just described crumbles under any kind of close inspection, and it ruins peace. The point of dating is to find out whether you and a woman are compatible for marriage; why would you wait to find out? As with all the advice about clarity in how you ask, it's better to know than to not know. Ambiguity destroys peace and serves no purpose in dating.

You're the man! (Both in the above scenario, and in the sense that your little league football coach says it.) If you want to avoid such a disastrous situation, ask the woman out soon. Ask her tomorrow! Ask her today! There are three main problems with the emotional build-up strategy. First, opportunities are missed when a man who *will* ask swoops in on your crush. If she's worth it, don't delay.

Second, often times the woman you think you're asking out actually only exists in your head. No woman is perfect, and it's unfair for that to be your standard. Do you want a woman to date you until you make your first mistake, then throw in the towel? Personally, I'd rather have a relationship based on mutual grace than one based on my qualifications. So initially, you think she's great. You're so scared to find out that she's not the perfect person you thought she was that you don't try to get to know her. Eventually you confess deep affection for someone you think is perfect because you were far enough

24

away to overlook the faults. How much better would it have been to develop the affection by getting to know a real woman?

The third problem is that the asking gets harder and harder. You become less and less willing to let go of the idea or the imaginary *relationship* (not woman) that you've grown attached to. Now when you ask her to coffee, it feels more like a marriage proposal. If I thought about every date like a marriage proposal, I would be paralyzed. I would lose my mind! The point of the first date is only to see if you want a second date.

Often in dating, people talk about "chemistry," so I'm going to borrow a concept from chemistry to explain this. Thermite is a mixture of aluminum and iron oxide that burns extremely hot. It burns so hot that to get it started, you have to light it with magnesium, which is itself a metal that only burns extremely hot. In chemistry, to get a reaction going requires *activation energy*. The fact that burning thermite is so difficult means it has an extremely high activation energy.

There's a reason you've never started a campfire using thermite. It's unnecessary, it's a pain, and it's definitely not the best way to get a long-lasting fire. Instead, you use a napkin or a paper towel, something with *low* activation energy. You start it with a match, then you slowly add bigger and bigger twigs and sticks, and then some logs. Dating should be the same way. Just strike a match and see if you can tend a fire that will last all evening. Don't go for a white-hot, specialized reaction that's difficult to get started.

We need good men to ask women on dates. We don't need any more "talking," or waiting, or hyper-emotional DTRs that come before any real action is taken. Just ask her out! It's only coffee! It's burning a napkin—no big deal. If you find that you don't ask her out given ample time and opportunity, you probably don't really want to date her.

Do you really like her?

Here are the only two questions that you need to answer to see if you should ask a woman out: 1) Is she cute? 2) Is she holy? The first question covers all practical attraction. If you are attracted to someone's personality, she will become physically attractive to you as you spend time together. The second question covers the matter of character. Don't waste time dating someone whom you know for sure doesn't have the same values as you. If you're a Christian, you don't ask non-Christians on dates.

There are plenty of women for whom I can answer "yes" to the first question; they're fun and smart and pretty. But an answer of "yes" to the first question is not enough. Dating a woman only because she's attractive, even if it's more than physical attraction, is a recipe for disaster. Do what you can to discern where she is in life and where she's heading to see if it matches up well enough with where you want to be. Avoid the pain of getting romantically involved with a woman whom you know isn't right for you.

There are also plenty of women for whom I rejoice in answering "yes" to the second question; they love the Lord, they serve others humbly, they're admired by their friends, they're sweet. Part of me *wants* to have a crush on them, but I simply don't. I avoid stirring up the hearts of these admirable women by not asking them on dates, if I know for sure we aren't compatible.

But there *she* is, hammocking in the overlap region of the Venn diagram that I have just described. She's cute, she's holy, she's probably out of your league. (That's a good thing, because who wants to date a woman who's just "gettable"?) If you can confidently answer yes to both questions, stop waiting! If you really like her, you will ask her out. Go for it! Have your friends help you get fired up! This is one of my favorite stages, so if you need a pre-game pump-up talk, give me a call or text! (405) 443-7227. *dang*

There's a quote I like from a movie called "We Bought a Zoo," which Matt Damon's character, Benjamin Mee, uses to make the best decisions in his life, including meeting his wife and buying a family zoo.

"Sometimes all you need is twenty seconds of insane courage. Just literally twenty seconds of embarrassing bravery and I promise you, something great will come of it."

Just go to her contact and hit "call"; once the phone is ringing, there's no going back!

In eighth grade, I had the biggest crush on a girl named Rylee. She sat behind me in US History. After making a plan for a date (with my mom's help), I worked up the nerve to ask her out. My insane courage only lasted for about four seconds, as after class I turned around and said "Hey…" After an awkward pause, she said "Yes?" and I invited her to the movies. All it took was four seconds of insane courage—a spark that started a fire—and now we're married! That was a joke. None of my stories in this book end in "now we're married." She said no, but it was probably the bravest thing I'd ever done.

I met a woman in the dining hall in college, and she seemed really fun and cool. A few days later, I saw her studying in an area of the library where absolutely no talking is allowed. After my boy gave me a pump-up speech in a different part of the library, I walked back in with a note. There she was! I could still turn back. I sat

That's not weird at all [handwritten note]

down, gathered my thoughts, took a deep breath, and started my twenty-second clock. Then I walked over to her, handed her the note, and waited for her to read it. Then she gave me her number! I confidently share both of those stories because just asking is such a good thing. When I see either of these two ladies around, I'm not at all embarrassed to talk with them. All it took was 20 seconds of insane courage, the strike of a match to start asking. You can do it!

I'll make you a deal. If there was a woman in your mind as you read this section, ask her out right now, and I'll ask out the woman who was in my mind as I wrote it. I'm not joking. I'm going to call her right now, and if everything goes as well as I hope, I'll meet you in Planning a Date.

3. Planning a Date: Thoughtfulness is Key

As the title of this chapter may suggest, planning a great date mostly requires thoughtfulness. Giving the effort to *think* when planning a date makes all the difference, and it requires practically no skill. It's pretty simple, really: take time to consider what your date would want, and then let those conclusions affect your planning. More on this throughout the chapter.

So, how did asking go?! I'll tell you how it went on my end. I called. This sister *doesn't have voicemail*, so we played phone tag a couple of rounds and then finally talked. We caught up and chatted a bit, then I went to the point and asked her if she would be interested in going a date. She said yes! Here's what impressed me: she communicated *so* clearly. Instead of leaving it as "yes," she explained that she would prefer something simpler like coffee for the first date rather than a full meal.

She was right: the first few

Thoughtfulness starts with considering the level of commitment a date requires. In other words, driving an hour each way to a 5-course meal at a nice restaurant is not a very considerate first date. You don't know how comfortable conversation will be, you don't know whether she wants to spend four hours with you, and you don't want her to feel trapped.

That's why the first few dates should be simple and flexible. Particularly if you're going on a date with a woman who is practically a stranger, both for her sake and yours, make it as low pressure as possible. Try coffee or dessert. If you don't know her, consider meeting there, rather than picking her up, so she feels like she can leave whenever she wants to. Have plans with other people that start a couple of hours after your date, so there's an end in sight. Let the first date occur during daylight hours. She may or may not notice these considerations, but she'll appreciate them in feeling more relaxed on your date.

For the first date, a shared snack or drink is easy, expected (in a good way), and low pressure. Coffee or dessert or a quick midday meal are good options for first dates because they are necessarily variable in length. You can practically drink a cup of coffee as quickly as you want, certainly in no longer than fifteen minutes. That's what makes "getting coffee" ideal: we can sit here and enjoy our coffee (ice cream, pie, etc.) for twenty minutes and talk, and then move on if we're uncomfortable. Or if conversation is flowing and things are going well, we can take small sips and then stay around even after the excuse is gone.

Either way, try to have something planned for after the date. No matter how well the first date is going, it doesn't need to last more than about 2 hours start-to-finish. Don't try to prolong it into an evening thing or tack on additional activities. The measure of a good first date is not a long first date, it's a second date. You would rather her leave thinking about how much fun she's having and how she would like to do this again rather than about how long the date has taken. The same goes for your own thinking, actually. Leave the date with the expectation that there's more good to come.

Plan more than one date

Whenever you propose the specific date plan to her, whether that be when you pick her up or when you agree upon a time and place to meet, have at least one back-up plan in mind. That way, the conversation either goes something like:

You: "Do you like coffee?"

Date: "I love it! I'm practically addicted."

You: "Perfect! I was thinking we could try [name of specific coffee shop (not the one she normally goes to)], does that sound alright?"

Date: "Ooh that sounds great, I've been meaning to try that place."

Or:

You: "Are you a coffee drinker?"

Date: "Hmm, it's not my favorite..."

You: "That's funny! Well I was thinking we could try out [insert name of ice cream/tea/dessert shop]. How does that sound?"

Date: "Ooh that sounds great, I've been meaning to try that place."

Hopefully you can see how having even more than two ideas in mind would be helpful. What if she doesn't like tea or coffee, or if she's lactose intolerant? Go to a bakery, or get a smoothie.

Once when I took a woman on a date which was not our first date, I thought of three or four different dinner options with varying levels of "adventurousness." When it came time to eat, I held out my hands spread apart and asked, "How adventurous are you feeling?" She indicated that she was somewhere in the middle of the scale, so we

31

went to my second-most-adventurous option. Thinking of more than one date idea allows for a flexible, fun date.

The point of flexibility is to prevent the awkwardness that comes with breaking a rigid plan. One time, I picked a woman up for date and I was hungry! The plan was to eat lunch and then go to a park for a while. When I asked her whether she was ready to eat, she responded like it was the strangest idea she'd heard all week. It was easy enough to just flip the order of the date—frisbee golf at the park first, then lunch—so it ended up being no big deal.

The most important thing is to actually think of date ideas. It's not only poor form but rude to pick a woman up for a date and say, "So what do you want to do?" While this may seem like the ultimate form of flexibility, it's actually just a lack of forethought and effort. When I offered my date varying levels of "adventure" with our meal, she had the fun of open possibilities without the stress of choice, and she knew that I had been thoughtful enough to pick a couple of restaurants she would like. A woman will feel honored that you took the time to plan a date for her and relaxed that she doesn't have to make decisions and be judged for them. Later on in a relationship, it's good to take turns planning dates, but in the early stages, you need to put in the effort to think of a plan (or two, or three) and be flexible enough to change it.

Thoughtfulness: YOU can do it

The necessity of planning a date rather than leaving it unstructured is the beginner level of thoughtfulness. Here's the thing about thoughtfulness: most guys can tell you what a good date would look like. Take a minute and just think of a cheesy, over-the-top great date. You bring roses, you take her to her favorite nice restaurant (or cook a candlelit dinner for her, maybe picnic). You walk somewhere scenic and watch the sun set. You bring her favorite dessert. There may be some occasion for fireworks, I don't know. The point is, most of the good stuff is cliché by now, right? It's not too difficult to think of what would be a great, romantic date.

Now dial it *way* down. Don't bring a dozen roses, but what woman wouldn't appreciate a flower you stole from a bush on the way to pick her up? You can think of which restaurants have a variety of menu options so she'll find something she likes, and which ones aren't so expensive that she'll feel uncomfortable letting a relative stranger buy her meal. You know a park or an area of town for a nice walk, or you can drive around a bit before you pick her up to scout one out. In the early stages, you don't know her favorite dessert, but you can think ahead and bring your favorite dessert to share.

Thoughtfulness is not that hard, and it's especially critical for men like me—I'm not very good at flirting, and I'm not very smooth. It's where hard work and planning and guts beat talent every time. I say "guts" because sometimes you can come up with what would be a great idea for a date, but you're too scared of being "over-the-top" (read: vulnerable) to actually execute it. There are some among us who are always smooth, or who are creative enough to come up with more perfect and fun dates than the rest of us ever could. But thoughtfulness is something that anyone, even *you*, can use to make the woman you invite out feel honored, and to make a date go well.

The distinguishing point with thoughtfulness is to ensure that your preparation is truly for *her*. On an early date, some things (like anything in the first paragraph of this section) are more unsettling than sweet. If you feel a sense of desperation to impress your date, it is most likely self-motivated. In this case, you only care to have her like you, rather than simply caring for her. However, I'd encourage you to not spend too much time thinking about this distinction. If in doubt, make the pursuit about her, and go for it!

Tailored

Another way of being thoughtful is to customize your date ideas to your date. Personally, I would find it a bit weird to go on the exact same date with two different women. This doesn't exclude eating at the same restaurants or doing similar activities, but a start-to-finish copy of a date seems almost disingenuous. More than that, a copied date is probably less effective, in terms of getting to know the woman you're taking.

By the time you're planning activity-based dates, you should already know some things about the woman you're inviting from when you got coffee or dessert together. Here's where you can come up with a specific activity that you think she would enjoying participating in alongside you. Just because this idea is custom-made does not mean it has to be elaborate; if she loves horses, your third date could be a rodeo or an equestrian match. It should not be a guided horse-ride on the beach (save that for an anniversary!). Don't take your outdoorsy date to a symphony concert; don't take your bookworm date mountain biking.

The purpose of a tailored date is two-fold: first, it should be fun. You want the woman you ask to enjoy spending time with you, and a fun activity helps with that, if it's fun for both of you. Don't do something that bores you to death just to impress her; you will probably come off as bored and boring. More than that, she won't really get the opportunity to learn anything about you if you're doing something you don't care to do. That leads to the second purpose of a tailored date. You will learn more about your romantic interest doing something she really enjoys—somewhere that she's in her element, relaxed. The point of dating is to get to know one another, so plan a date where she can enjoy being herself, and one that's fun enough that she'll want to go on another!

On the point of getting to know her: be sure that your first several dates are ones in which you can talk freely. Discussion is the easiest way to learn about someone, so a date that limits discussion is ineffective. Couples who are together for a long time say things like, "Isn't it great when you can just be around someone and not have to talk, to just enjoy being together?" That's all well and good, but it takes some serious time to develop! Dates without talking are for couples who need a few hours away from the kids to just breathe and be quiet. They already know one another. That said, for the first couple of dates, don't take a woman to the movies where you sit in silence for a couple of hours and then drop her off. A movie date is overly-simple, not tailored or thoughtful, and pretty ineffective for getting to know someone.

Good to great

To take a date to the next level in terms of quality, it should include a shared meal or snack, and it should be collaborative or fresh. The first part is easy, but there's something about eating together that's much deeper than what it seems on the surface. Be sure to plan the timing of the date around the meal if you intend to eat together. That is, don't pick her up at 4:45 pm for dinner, and don't plan something at 6:00 pm if you're not going to eat together. Eating together is also a great time for conversation, first because there's nothing else to do, and second because the rhythm of chewing and talking requires a somewhat balanced conversation.

Great dates are also collaborative or fresh. Any date that establishes a unique shared experience is better than one that feels like any other day. A "collaborative" date is one that requires you and your romantic interest to work together, to create something new or to overcome a challenge. Not only is this style of date fun and impactful, but it also helps to show off the character of the person whom you are trying to know. For instance, after I made the canoe I referenced in Why We Date, my date and I paddled it on a river near where we live. Tandem canoeing is challenging (particularly in a boat built by an amateur), so we had to work together to navigate and trust one another to not capsize. Working together to overcome the challenge of canoeing was fun, and it also showed off my date's willingness to get into a sinking boat, which I really admired.

A "fresh" date includes a new experience, however simple. With the woman I called at the end of the last chapter, we went to a local coffee shop that only recently opened up. She had not tried it before, and neither had I, so we got to try a new place together. Trying a new coffee shop is nothing extraordinary, but it's still more fun than going to the same old place. Now I may remember the date any time the new place comes up in conversation with my friends. A fresh date may also be an interesting concert or something educational like a cooking class. Trying or learning something new on your date will make it stand out, and it provides a shared experience which you can build off of in conversation as you move forward in a relationship. A creative experience, like making art, is necessarily fresh, because you make something new every time. It's even better if you collaborate to make something new.

Let's take a step back. While I delight in challenging guys to think of fun, unique dates, I want to say I think it's more important by far that you go on the date at all, that you be sincere, and that you genuinely try to know a woman and to be known by her. At the end of the day, a great date probably won't make or break her liking you. The point of thoughtfulness in planning a date is to show that you care for and respect the woman you are taking out, and to make it easier to have fun. If you are confident that you and your date will enjoy your time together, you can relax.

As with most of this book, this practical advice is not the most important part of dating—finding a wife is. But I get frustrated sometimes when I hear dating advice like this: "Oh, just keep walking with God and doing your thing, and it will all work out." On the macro scale, I believe that to be true, but what do I do about it tomorrow? What do I do when an opportunity with an awesome lady arises, and I want to embrace it well? I think putting a lot of consideration into a date is a good step after asking a woman out. You neither want to stress as if it all depends on your preparation nor be so nonchalant as to be wasteful and disrespectful of time and emotional capital.

With that said, I'm going to tack on to this chapter a short list of date ideas to get your thinking going. Some of these I have done in part or in whole; most of them, I would be glad to try. None of them are complete date ideas, so use your own thoughtfulness to customize these ideas or to think of new ones. It is necessary that you consider whether your date, as an individual, would enjoy these ideas or just feel uncomfortable. Cross reference this list with what you heard from her on your earlier dates. Don't shy away from physically active dates, but if you plan one, be sure to give her a heads-up so she can dress accordingly. Don't throw away a thoughtful, fun idea just because it doesn't jump out as either collaborative or fresh.

(C) – collaborative
(F) – fresh

- Canoe to a restaurant (C, F)
- Escape rooms (C)
- Try a new restaurant or dessert spot (F)
- Cooking class (F)
- Disc Golfing (F)
- Take a guest lesson from a karate studio (F)
- Painting/pottery/art class (F)
- Explore a new area of the city (C, F)
- Karaoke (duet!) (C)
- Photography in a scenic area (F)
- Try a new recipe (C, F)
- Ride bikes in the park
- Go to a local band's concert (F)
- Check out a museum (F)

The juices are flowing. Nail down a plan (and a back-up plan, and consider a back-up to the back-up plan). Eat or drink together, try something new, and let it be somewhere you can talk. Think through the level of involvement: is it appropriate for how comfortable you are together? When you've got the plan ready and it's the day to execute it, Make it Happen, Cap'n.

4. Make it Happen, Cap'n

You don't have time to be reading this! I'll keep it brief. The date is today and we're excited! Here's what you should do to get ready. Be sure to leave yourself enough time to complete everything from this list that you want to, and then to breathe and pick her up.

The date is in three hours!
Okay, breathe. You have time. Go clean your car. The interior matters more than the exterior, but if you have time, do both. If there's a smell, drive with the windows down to air it out. [Note: leave the windows up on the date so she doesn't worry about her hair.] Vacuum, wash the outside if necessary. Throw away the trash. She will notice, even though she probably won't say anything. This is just like planning a date—the thought and effort you put in now will make things go better even if she doesn't consciously notice. Besides, she'll probably consciously notice. Either way, you'll be more confident picking her up if your car is clean.

Okay, that's done. Do you stink? DO NOT ATTEMPT TO MASK IT WITH FRAGRANCE. Take a shower. You have to be pretty fresh to not need a shower, particularly if you are reading this and you are 21 years old or younger. Just take a shower. Again, she'll notice, and it will matter for your confidence. While you're at it, just run through the full hygiene regimen. Brush your teeth, even if you're about to eat. If you shave, shave. If you wear a beard or other facial hair, make sure it's cleaned up around the edges. Use extra antiperspirant. It's not out of bounds to put a small amount of antiperspirant on your palms if your

39

hands sweat a lot, particularly if you intend to dance. Put on a clean set of clothes (in both senses of the word "clean"). Wear the nicer end of your normal look; don't try to change things up too much right now wardrobe-wise or you'll get distracted wondering about it. Check the weather. If it might be chilly, lean on the side of wearing a jacket (to share or to cover up your sweating pits).

Breathe. Pray about the date. Philippians 4:6-7 (NIV) says, "Do not be anxious about anything, but in *every* situation, by prayer and petition, with thanksgiving, present your requests to God. And the peace of God, which transcends all understanding, will guard your hearts and your minds in Christ Jesus" (emphasis added). God wants you to pray about every situation you might be anxious about, even if it's a date. There's not a prayer that's too petty for God if it's an honest prayer about your concerns.

Take a second to think of some conversation starters. I prefer questions about real life. Ask about her day or her week like you're a normal human being. Try to remember some things she said she was looking forward to during your earlier conversations so you can ask how they went. Then again, it can be good to ask a goofy question to break the ice also: how many holes does a straw have? Coke or Pepsi, and why? It is highly unlikely that you will need to consciously refer to this mental exercise during your date, but again: confidence.

Call your friend and/or your mom or dad and ask for encouragement. They're not going to tell you anything they haven't already told you, but it's good to hear it all again. This is your last chance to remember who's on your team like in "Why We Date."

If you decided to snag a flower or her favorite drink on the way, be sure to leave time to do it. You're ready, you're excited, you've got time. Breathe.

When it comes down to it, the things on the list below are closer to honors than obligations. Sometimes I think of having a girlfriend in terms of these little obligations. I want a reason to keep my car clean. I want an excuse to shave my neck more than once a week. Are those the only reasons I want a girlfriend? No! I want a wife, and a girlfriend is a healthy intermediate step. I want to find a woman to spend my life with and for. (Notice I say "spend" and not "live." My wife will never be my purpose—she can't handle that. However, I'm called to love God, and God says I should love my wife in a way that is costly to myself. I will spend my life *for* her in that I will love her sacrificially, but not in a way that my identity is found in her.) Maybe I would attract a woman more easily if I did these little duties on my own. I should probably have a better attitude about them in general, but without a good reason, cleaning my car just never seems to make it to the top of the priority list.

The Date is in Three Hours Checklist:

- ☐ Clean car
- ☐ (Obtain flower or drink)
- ☐ Shower
- ☐ Brush teeth
- ☐ Apply deodorant
- ☐ Shave or trim facial hair
- ☐ Check weather
- ☐ Map the drive to pick her up
- ☐ Conversation starters
- ☐ Pump-up talk from friend
- ☐ Pray
- ☐ Breathe

THE DATE IS HAPPENING RIGHT NOW

Put the book down and talk to her! That's a joke. Of course you should read this section *before* you go.

You've got plenty of time. You've mapped how long it takes to pick her up, and if you're like me, you'll probably leave early. Now this may seem counter-intuitive, but it's ideal to be three to four minutes late. You're not going to a job interview that you need to be early for to impress the employer. Women (at least the women in my family) will take the full amount of time they have to get ready. They know when you're coming, and they may feel a bit rushed to be ready by then. At your scheduled time, they will wait with anticipation. This gives them a couple of minutes to relax a bit and then to get excited for the date. For the record, I am not just making this up. My aunt (who *knows*) gave me this advice. "Five minutes late is rude, four minutes late is good." It's difficult for me to execute. I've been near where I needed to be and parked the car and played a song just so I would slow down and wait. Whatever you do, don't be early. [Important note: this advice does not apply to dates where you're meeting at an agreed-upon location.]

You don't have to drive to pick her up if you've carefully planned your date to be comfortably walkable. Make sure she knows ahead of time that you intend to walk so she can choose shoes accordingly. If a car is necessary for your date plan but you don't have one, borrow one from your parents or from a friend that trusts you. There's something about being picked up that matters to a woman. You're also in for some serious cred if you went to the extra effort of borrowing a car.

Get out of the car and go to her door, if possible. While texting to confirm the date and to find out her address is perfectly fine, texting her "Here" instead of going to the door is egregious and unacceptable. Some people in locked apartment buildings find it easier to meet at the lobby; still, go to the lobby. In this case, call to let her know that you're ready to pick her up. Open the car door for her. Depending on her expectations, you may open the car door for her to get out, too, but I find there are very few young women who expect this unless you say something. At any rate, it's almost never awkward to open the door for her to get in. Open all the building doors for her throughout the whole date, even if it means taking a step ahead, except the door to her house (of course). If she mentions that you don't have to open doors for her or that she's capable of doing it herself, it's okay to say something like, "I know you *can* open the door for yourself. I just want to!"

It's good to offer her sincere, simple compliments. Don't be crass or creepy about her appearance. Avoid being vague.

Creepy: "You're so beautiful, I could just watch you all day."

"Girl, you're thicker than a bowl of oatmeal." *eww*

Vague: "You're nice."

Good: "I love your laugh!" "You have such a kind smile."

Be sure you're complimenting her honestly, and for her sake, not your own. Compliment her personality, too. "I think you're hilarious" goes just as well for her esteem, if not better, than "your hair looks really pretty."

Pay for the date, whether it's for coffee or for admission to the zoo. If she's confused about why you want to pay, you were probably not clear enough in asking her out. This and picking her up are two distinguishing factors of a date. If one of my friends wonders whether she just went on a "real date," I ask three questions: "Did he drive? Did he pay? Did he call it a date?" Be upfront and clear about your intention to pay whenever the service-person asks. Tip generously without being overt. Be kind to wait staff without being insincere.

Relax. Listen to her instead of thinking of the next related story you're about to tell. If she hesitates that she's talking too much, actively encourage her that you want to hear the whole story, all of her stories, anything she wants to say. Be honest without oversharing so she can get to know the real you. Do not spend twenty minutes telling her your life story; if she asks, give her the 4 minutes and thirty seconds version, and she may ask follow-up questions. Don't feel pressure to be someone you're not; how tragic would it be for her to develop a huge crush on a guy who's not you, but who she thinks is you? Ask intentional questions: "Do you have any siblings? What do you enjoy doing besides work/school? What kind of music do you like?"

When it's time to drop her off, open her car door and walk her to the door. Don't overextend the date [see "Planning a Date"]. Express that you had fun; thank her for coming. Don't promise something you're unsure of. Once you're sure that you want to pursue her longer-term, you can say things like, "I'd love to do this again sometime soon" or "I'll call you tomorrow!"

This is not the moment where you see what kind of "progress" you can make in terms of physicality. Any physical affection shown should be for her sake and not for your own—in one direction. Be aware that all physical displays of affection will make your decision-making process chemically more difficult. A quick hug or side-hug or a kiss on the cheek are the most you want to do. Read her body language and ensure that you are not doing anything that will make her even the slightest bit uncomfortable. If you're in doubt, just wave and walk away; there's not a rule anywhere that says you have to end a date with a kiss. If you're offended by the preceding paragraph, be sure to read "Why We Date." If you're still offended, check your motivations, pray about it, and then make your own decisions.

Make sure she gets into her house without any problems, then drive away and smile.

It Just Happened, Cap'n (day of the date)

So how did it go? Sometimes it takes a while for me to find out how I feel about a date. One time I went on a date with a woman, and everything logistical worked out quite ideally. There weren't a bunch of awkward lulls in conversation. We laughed together and learned about one another. We ate cupcakes and watched the sunset in a really cool area. But at the end of the date, I wasn't very excited about it. There didn't seem to be much spark between us. There weren't very many things I could point out to say "this is something great about her."

However, as I talked about the date with my mom and with my friends, I got more and more excited about it. I remembered things we'd discussed and admirable traits started to emerge. By about 24 hours after the date, I was psyched. This woman was awesome! (Unfortunately, that was just in time for summer break.)

Ultimately, all you need to decide right now is whether you'd like to take her on another date. Take the rest of the night to decide. If it was your first date and it wasn't terrible, lean toward a second date; not everyone opens up in meaningful ways during the first time you're around them. That doesn't mean they're not worth knowing. Talk about your date with your friends and family to help you process. In my experience, if you want to be prompted to recap the date in greater detail, talk through it with your girl friends or your mom.

Periodically check if you're thinking about the date and if you're smiling when you do. Once, I determined that I probably wasn't into dating a certain woman because we spent time together on a Friday evening and it was Sunday before I remembered that it had happened. That's a pretty sure sign that there was nothing special going on there.

If it's honest, communicate simply to your date that you enjoyed the time you spent together. This is the one aspect of early dating that I find allowable to communicate by text, but it should not turn into a whole conversation. Something like "Hey [Name of Your Crush]! Thank so much for getting coffee with me today; I had a lot of fun!" works quite well. [Side note to all my grammar friends out there: these first texts are a great opportunity to show off your mastery of the semi-colon and long-dash. Just saying.] If she responds with a "Me too! Thanks for inviting me!" then you're all done. Maybe "like" the message if you have iMessage, or say something like "Have a good night!" Don't reply with a conversation-starter like "I'm glad. What are you up to for the rest of the night?" Let the date end; let the conversation you already had speak for itself. The conversation may get better in her head as it percolates. It's also good to call her to express something like the above, but less advised if you're not sure whether you'd like to ask her out again. In any case, I'd save a call for the next day (and no later).

The Next Day

Alright, you've taken your time to decide. The day after the date and no later, you need to call her and communicate. Are you up for another date? If yes, refer to "Asking for a Date." Call her and catch up a bit. Reference conversation you've had with her. At this point, do *not* listen to any kind of thought that assumes she will not want to hear from you or go on another date. It's your job to ask; it's her job to say "no" if that's how she feels. But we're hoping she'll say yes! If she does, review "Planning a Date," and pay extra attention to the idea of using what you learn from your previous date to plan your next one! If she mentioned wanting to ride bikes in the park, go ride bikes in the park! If she loves soccer, go watch a soccer match. Thoughtfulness isn't complex!

As with the planning stage, the advice in this section is never make-or-break. A woman who likes you will overlook your disheveled hair or the crumbs on your floorboard, but you don't want her to need to. A woman who does not like you probably won't start just because you vacuumed your car and brushed your teeth. Either way, she will probably notice the effort you put in to the date, whether consciously or unconsciously.

The way I'm wired, I need something to *do*. How can I contribute? How can I make the date the best possible? I think the advice in this chapter is just about as practical as it gets in terms of executing a successful date— one where there are no stumbling blocks to getting to know a woman better. If I follow these guidelines for a date and she's still not into me, I know I gave it my best shot, and there are less doubts and what-ifs moving forward. Don't worry about that too much.

At any rate, if you did what you could and went on the date, and you just aren't feeling it, or if you asked her for another date and she's not feeling it, then unfortunately the next chapter is for you.

5. Over It

Look, dating stinks, but it's good. It's hard to get your hopes up and then let them go repeatedly. That's just part of the deal, and it's still a good deal. It's still worth it. But you don't have to be ecstatic about how you feel during every stage of the dating process.

You're over it

Maybe she's great, but just not great for you. Maybe you learned something about her or about yourself that means your lives are heading in completely different directions. Maybe you realized you just aren't having very much fun with her when you spend time together. Maybe you don't want to date her anymore, but you're scared to let go of this potential relationship because you can't be sure another will come along. Even still, for one reason or another, you're over it.

It's fine to feel bummed that a relationship didn't work out, even if you're the one who ended it. Ultimately, she deserves better than to date someone who doesn't have a crush on her, right? If you can tell a relationship isn't going anywhere, go ahead and end any romantic aspect of it. You're not "letting her down easy" by slowly drifting away; you're making it more painful for all parties involved.

As clear as you were in asking her out, be even clearer in breaking off the romantic pursuit. Text—again— is unacceptable for this. If you've been on a couple of dates but it never developed into anything serious, still call her. At the very least, call and leave a voicemail. This is better by far than just never calling or offering any closure with regard to your intentions. I have walked away from conversations like these smiling because I know I did what needed to be done, and feeling the release of tension that had previously existed between my intentions and her understanding of my intentions. Strangely enough, sometimes a conversation ending a relationship feels good in some of the same ways that asking a woman out feels good. I expressed myself clearly; I respected her feelings in the way I communicated. I did the right thing.

Ending a dating relationship is simply part of dating. It shouldn't be a huge deal. Neither party is necessarily saying the other is a bad person or a bad spouse, only that the two parties aren't ideal for one another. There are plenty of women I would encourage my friends to date whom I had the privilege of taking on dates before finding out we wouldn't make a good couple. If dating is to check compatibility for a spouse, unless a relationship ends in marriage, someone will likely realize sooner than the other that it won't work out. That person should say so. If you find out first, you're not the bad guy for ending the relationship, you're the guy who does what he implicitly agreed to do by going on dates in the first place.

If you are in a more-developed dating relationship and within driving range of one another, you should break things off in-person. Unless you've been "official" for several months, here's a decent way to end things: ask if you can meet her somewhere public-ish, like a café. You don't want to embarrass her by having others overhear the conversation, but neither do you want to have a difficult conversation in the emotional space of a one-on-one, private setting. Ask to meet midday, when you know she still has further obligations in the day. She will be less likely to take it unnecessarily hard if she has other things to spend her effort on. Be clear and gentle in explaining that you don't see the relationship going further. Avoid explaining why; the last thing you want is for her to think of your ideal spouse as *the* ideal spouse. Express in as few words as necessary your appreciation for her as a person and for the dating relationship, then cordially end the conversation.

Don't rush into trying to be friends. Especially if you're the one who ended things, be as gentle and considerate as possible in re-establishing contact. In incidental interactions, be friendly, not awkward. It shouldn't be awkward after a couple of weeks.

Hear this: the only time "ghosting" is acceptable is if you are literally dead. At any stage of a dating relationship, if you see fit to end it, taking responsibility for that opinion and communicating it clearly in the kindest way possible is always the best option. If you end relationships well, you don't accumulate a list of people you have to avoid! You don't limit your possibilities for who you can have as friends. This is the better way! But you won't always be the one to end it.

She's Over It

In my case, I'm rarely the one to end things! This is partly a by-product of me being the initiator of most dating relationships I pursue. Typically if I'm willing to ask a woman out, I'm up for taking her on dates until she sees something I can't.

So how do you know when she's over it? First of all, present her with plenty of opportunities to express her feelings about your relationship, the easiest type being a clear invitation for a date. If you present her with a clear yes or no question, it's easier for her to give you a clear answer. A woman does not owe you anything in terms of dating—not one thing—but if there were one thing, it would be an honest and clear "no." I wish all women were mature enough to think this way, but unfortunately that is not the case. For all the same reasons you initially shy away from breaking things off in a clear way, she feels the same way about refusing your invitation to a date. Most of the time this looks like a long string of plans not working out. If you offer specific opportunities to spend time together and she always seems to be busy and makes no effort to reschedule, she probably doesn't like you. Think of the lengths to which you are willing to go to be around someone you're interested in romantically. If she liked you, she would make it happen. Even still, it's better to ask for a clear answer.

Asking for a clear answer doesn't have to be difficult. A few months ago, I took a woman on a couple of dates, and I could tell she was hesitant about the idea of going on another date, despite having expressed different feelings earlier. I asked her out for some time during the weekend, and she explained that she was busy without making any attempt to reschedule or expressing much appreciation. All I said was something like, "Oh that sounds fun! For clarity's sake, though, is another date something you think you would be up for?" And it was enough of a prompt for her to express how she was feeling. The only hurt I felt was that she likely would have let me go on asking her out until I essentially told myself no. If you are a woman reading this, please be kind in offering a clear end to a dating pursuit.

Unless your first dating relationship ends in marriage, ending dating relationships is as much a part of dating as beginning them. It makes sense that all but one of your dating relationships will come to an end. As I said earlier, normally one person finds out that a relationship would not be good for marriage before the other realizes it.

Attraction (in the sense of enjoying being around someone) is a perfectly acceptable predictor of compatibility. We're on a team to find out whether we would make a good marriage. She found out first that we wouldn't. I can't lie to you, and I wouldn't, it stinks *way* more when she's over it than when you are.

Dating stinks, but it's good. I only want to date someone who has a crush on me; as much as it hurts, I hope that any dating relationship where the woman doesn't have a crush on me comes to an end. Of course, I would rather her just have a crush on me. But since I care for her, I also want her to date someone she's compatible with, even if it's not me.

The pain of desiring relationship, of hoping for a specific relationship, is not something to rush through or ignore. No matter how briefly or long a dating relationship lasts, when it ends, there's a disappointment of what you hoped for. In reality, you did not lose anything; you only lost the hope for something that might have been. In fact, you gained progress in what you are actually searching for, but that's not what you want to hear right now.

It didn't work out

She's over it, or you asked her on a first date and she said no. Bummer. What do you do?

First, let yourself think about it. Often, my mind wants to come up with ways that it might still work out. I've learned to allow those kinds of thoughts. I know from experience that they'll go away after a week or two. Importantly, I leave the hope in her hands—if she has been kind enough to express a clear end to the relationship, I'll leave it there unless she says something otherwise. If six months go by and I still think it would be a good idea to ask her out again, I'm willing to try it. Allowing that kind of thought with a long minimum time threshold for acting on it is a healthy way of validating it without causing unnecessary pain. By the way, this isn't crazy. I asked a woman on a date and she said no; it actually enabled me to relax and be myself around her. We developed a friendship once I was being myself, and after a while it seemed like a good idea to ask her again. Sure enough, she said yes. It didn't work out, but to this day I consider her to be a good friend.

You don't want to dwell on why it didn't work out—what you could have done differently or why she doesn't like you. Frankly, if you follow general common sense, you'll be in the ball park of her being able to fairly decide whether or not she wants to be in a relationship with you. Little can be done differently to sway a person's heart; often, what is done only prolongs the inevitable. Whatever you do, do not attempt to change who you are to be someone she wants to date. First of all, you are probably not capable of it. It's weird to change *for* another person. It makes her the center of your identity, in some sense. At any rate, you have no way of knowing what it is about you she would even change, so it would be a shot in the dark. Even if she does have a reason why she doesn't see your relationship working out, it's ultimately because she doesn't like you enough. If she did, she would be willing to risk other things to make it work. In short, you can't change an aspect of your character to make someone like you, and you shouldn't try to. Be who you are called to be, and trust that she might have all the respect in the world for you and simply not be interested in you romantically. And remember: you only need enough game for one girl. Maybe it didn't work out with this one, but it might with the next.

Express how you're feeling in a creative way. I like to write songs. Two of my favorite songs I've ever written

54

were written after dating relationships didn't work out. You may surprise yourself with how deeply something can resonate when you're writing about how you feel. It happens regularly that I'll write a song "inspired" by a situation and think *I feel something like this, but this is a bit of an overstatement.* Then through practicing the song, I find out just how truly it expresses what I mean. It's a little weird when that happens, but it's still good.

Write a song or a poem, even if it's bad. It may be like those two songs I mentioned above—a consolation prize: I'm bummed I don't have a dating relationship, but hey, at least I got some good art out of it. For that reason, don't feel any pressure to stop liking the art even after you think you should be over the girl. If it's good, it's good on its own. Don't show her whatever art you come up with. It's not for her, it's for you. It's really not even about her, in that it's actually about how you feel. But do share it with a friend you trust.

I think artistic expression is especially valuable after a dating relationship ends, because a dating relationship offers the hope of more beauty in life. When it doesn't work out, you can help make up for the lost hope by creating beauty through art or by observing beauty somewhere else. To this end, I've gone and sat in a library near where I live because it is known for its stunning architecture. If you enjoy nature, you can experience beauty in a river or a sunset or a forest. Ultimately, the beauty you see anywhere belongs to the God who made *her* beautiful, who makes relationships beautiful, and who makes everything beautiful in its time.

Press into good things, into beauty and into relationships with people whom you know love you and like you just for you. Don't let this be an occasion for destructive behavior; don't pursue a meaningless rebound relationship. Don't drink or do drugs to escape a feeling that will still be there until you *feel* it.

You can let it be an occasion for *constructive* behaviors. Go to the gym. Read the book you've been wanting to read. Work out your frustration on an exhausting run. While it's misguided to try to change for the woman you just pursued, there's nothing wrong with becoming a more desirable mate, more established as who you want to be. Knowing and being who you are may help you attract someone else. You want her to get to know your character and your heart, but big muscles don't hurt either (I'm allowed to say that because I don't have any).

Be Affected

Can I say this to you as a friend?: Nobody owes you a girlfriend, and nobody owes you anything to make up for your lack of a girlfriend. Even if the date went well, even if you were thoughtful and planned and drove and paid, even if she flirted with you, neither she nor anyone else owes you anything in the way of romantic relationship. The whole point of love is that you don't deserve it. You *can't*. Love you earn isn't love at all. The way to seek love out is to give it away, and that requires great cost.

But in spending of yourself, and in your desire for relationship, be encouraged that you're doing exactly what you're supposed to do. I think there's a common misconception among my friends that being affected by your desire for relationship is okay because it *will be* okay. That it's alright to be upset because eventually you'll get over it, and that one of these relationships will probably work out one day and then you'll be happy. I've come to believe that being affected by wanting a relationship—and I mean *wanting* it, so much that you want to yell sometimes and quit sometimes—is more than okay, it's *good*. It's good *now*. I see in the testimony of Scripture that I'm made to live in God's image, to look like Him, and He desires more than anything to give love away and to live in relationship. He would spend Himself for it. He *did* spend Himself for it, to make a way for us to be His. So I shouldn't feel any rush to get through the pain of desiring relationship.

As much as in feeling the sweetest joy, I can be assured that I'm alive in feeling the most aching desire. As humans and images of God, we're designed to feel and to be affected. In one of those two songs I mentioned earlier, I think the most important reminder to myself expresses that thought:

"I've been thinking, it's a good thing my heart still bleeds; 'cause you know that I want you, but I've got everything I need."

While I do believe pretty firmly that I'll have the privilege of being married one day, I can rest in the fact that I already have everything I require in terms of life and love.

To write any more than I already have would betray my experience, because this is as far as I've gotten: I know that God's love is better than life, and I know that for me, continuing to pursue marriage in dating is a very good thing.

Made in the USA
Lexington, KY
14 September 2018